FINANCIAL FOUNDATIONS FOR YOUNG ADULTS

BUILDING PERSONAL WEALTH AND SUCCESS

JIMBO SUSON

CONTENTS

DEDICATION

This book is for my wonderful wife, who has been a constant source of support and inspiration throughout this whole journey. Without her unwavering encouragement, advice, and trust in me, I would not have been able to write this book. Her love and understanding have made it possible for me to do what I love, which is to help people with their finances. I will always be grateful.

PREFACE

Welcome to the path to being in control of your money! As the author of this book, I bring you more than a decade of banking experience, a lot of financial knowledge, and a real desire to help people figure out the confusing world of personal finance. My goal has always been to give you the tools, information, and confidence you need to make smart decisions about your money, whether you're saving for a rainy day, investing in your future, or dealing with big life events.

When I think back to when I was young, I wish I had someone to help me avoid the traps and problems that come with handling money. I made my fair share of financial mistakes and failures because I didn't know much about this important part of life or how to handle it. From those battles, I've learned how to make sure that you, dear reader, don't have to go through the same ones.

Through this book, I want to give young adults like you the tools to take charge of your financial future by giving you easy-to-understand, practical tips and strategies. I hope that by sharing the lessons I've learned and the insights I've gained over the years, you will be better able to make good financial choices and build a strong foundation for long-term success.

So, let's go on this exciting journey together. Although I make no guarantees, I can say that after you finish reading this book, you'll be well on your way to becoming financially independent and living the life you've always wanted. Or at least have the knowledge.

Here's to your financial success!

Sincerely,

Jimbo Suson

Chapter 1.A

For long-term success and stability, it is important to start building a strong financial foundation early in life. When they move out into the real world, many young adults don't know how to handle their money well, which can cause stress, debt, and missed chances. This chapter is meant to give you the basic information and advice you need to build a strong financial foundation for the future.

- Understanding How Important it is to Handle Your Money

Managing money well is the most important part of personal finance and a key part of making sure you are financially stable. By learning how to handle money in a responsible way, you can make choices that will help your finances in the long run. Understanding the importance of money management means knowing how to make a budget, handle debt, save money, and invest. By getting good at these skills, you can avoid common money mistakes which will help you reach your goals faster, thus giving you a better life.

- Making decisions based on facts

One of the main benefits of knowing how to manage your money is being able to make smart decisions about your money. This means knowing when to save, spend, or invest, as well as how to make the best use of your money. When you make decisions based on good information, you can avoid making financial mistakes like taking on too much debt or investing in the wrong things.

- Getting to Your Financial Goals

You can set both short-term and long-term financial goals if you know how to handle your money well. Whether you want to save for a house down payment, start a business, or retire early, good money management lets you plan and work methodically toward your goals. This feeling of making progress and getting things done can give you more financial confidence and drive.

- Debt Management and Avoidance

Learning how to handle debt responsibly is also a part of knowing how to manage money. This means knowing how to use credit wisely, putting paying off debt at the top of your list, and staying away from high-interest debt. By managing your debt well, you can make sure that interest payments don't hurt your finances too much, improve your credit score, and feel less stressed about money.

- Freedom and financial security

For financial security and independence, it's important to learn how to handle money well. By making a budget, saving for emergencies, and investing for the future, you can build a stable financial foundation that will support you for the rest of your life. This feeling of security lets you follow your dreams, take calculated risks, and live a better life without constantly worrying about money.

- Less worry about money

One of the most important reasons to learn how to manage your money is to reduce financial stress. Stress about money can hurt your mental and physical health, your relationships, and your overall well-being. By taking care of your money well, you can get rid of this stress and focus on the things that really matter to you.

- Flexibility and the ability to change

Life is full of surprises, and sometimes things you didn't plan for can have a big effect on your finances. By learning how to manage your money, you can gain the flexibility and adaptability you need to deal with these problems. This could mean changing your budget, rethinking your financial goals, or coming up with creative ways to get around financial problems.

CHAPTER 1.B

S etting financial goals is a key part of getting your finances in good shape. By writing down your short-term and long-term goals, you create a road map that will help you make decisions about your money. This will allow you to use your resources wisely and make real progress toward financial success. This complete guide will show you how to set goals for your money that are realistic and doable.

- Check how your money is doing right now

Before you set financial goals, you should take account of how much you have right now. This means looking over your income, spending, savings, investments, and debts. If you know where you stand financially, you can set goals that are realistic and consider your unique situation.

- Figure out your priorities

Think about what's most important to you when it comes to money. This could mean paying off debt, saving for retirement, buying a home, or saving up for wedding or family. If you know what your priorities are, you can use your time and money on the things that are most important to you.

- Set goals for the short term and the long term

It's important to have both short-term and long-term goals when setting financial goals. Short-term goals usually have a time frame of one year or less, while long-term goals can take several years or even decades to reach. By setting both short-term and long-term goals, you can make small steps forward while keeping your eye on the bigger picture.

- Set goals that are SMART

Make sure your financial goals are SMART, which means they are specific, measurable, achievable, relevant, and have a time limit. What this means is:

1. Specific: To avoid confusion, be clear about what your goals are. For example, instead of saying you want to save more, say you want to save $5,000 in 12 months.

2. Measurable: Give your goal a number so you can keep track of your progress and know when you've reached it.

3. Achievable: Set goals that you can reach based on your current financial situation and how much money you could make in the future. Setting goals that are too big can make you feel disappointed and stop you from making progress.

4. Relevant: Make sure your goals are in line with your priorities and long-term goals to make sure they have meaning and help your overall financial health.

5. Time-bound: Set a deadline for your goals to make them more

urgent and get you to act. This also lets you divide your goals up into smaller, easier-to-achieve steps.

- Make a plan of what to do

Once you know what your financial goals are, you can plan to reach them. This could mean making a budget, saving more, investing, or cutting back on expenses. Figure out the steps you need to take to reach each goal and make a promise to do them regularly.

- Keep track of your progress

Make sure you stay on track with your financial goals by checking in on them often. This could mean looking at your budget, keeping track of your savings, or judging how well your investments are doing. Keeping track of your progress lets you make changes when you need to and celebrate your successes along the way.

- Change and keep track of your goals

As your finances and priorities change, you should be ready to change and update your goals. Things like getting married, having kids, or changing careers can have a big effect on your financial goals. Check your goals often to make sure they are still important and attainable.

CHAPTER 1.C

P utting together a budget is a key part of being financially successful. A well-made budget helps you keep track of your income and
spending, so you can make sure you don't spend more than you earn
and put money toward your financial goals. In this step-by-step guide,
I'll share with you how to make a budget that works for you and changes
as your finances do.

- Find out how much you make each month

Start by figuring out how much money you make each month from
all sources. This includes your salary, money you make from freelancing, rent, and any other regular income you get. If your income changes
from month to month, figure out an average by adding up what you've
made over the past six to twelve months.

- List Your Fixed Expenses

Fixed expenses are monthly costs that don't change much from
month to month. Rent or mortgage payments, utility bills, insurance
premiums, and loan payments are all examples of fixed expenses. Write

down all of your fixed expenses and how much they cost.

- List Your Variable Expenses

Costs that change from month to month are called variable expenses. They are usually based on how much you use or consume. Costs like groceries, eating out, entertainment, clothes, and transportation are all examples of variable costs. Estimate how much you spend each month on each variable expense based on how you've been spending recently.

- Determine Your Spending Limits

Now that you've made a list of all your income and expenses, give each category of variable expenses a spending limit. This will help you decide how to spend your money and make sure you don't spend more than you can afford. Be realistic when you set limits on how much you can spend, but also push yourself to find ways to save money.

- Set aside money for your financial goals

To get closer to your financial goals, put some of your income toward savings or paying off debt. Depending on your goals and financial situation, this can be a fixed amount or a percentage of your income. Set priorities for your goals and make sure your budget shows how much you want to reach them.

- Keep track of your money

Check your spending often to stay on track with your budget. This can be done with a spreadsheet, a budgeting app, or even pen and paper. By keeping track of your spending, you can find patterns, find places where you might be spending too much, and make changes as needed.

- Check and change your budget

Your budget should change as your financial situation does. Review your budget often to make sure it is still relevant and useful. This could mean changing how much you can spend, putting money toward different financial goals, or recalculating your income. You can stay on track for financial success if you keep a budget that changes with your needs and priorities.

In addition, you can check out my Budgeting 101 book on Amazon.

CHAPTER 1.D

To be financially stable and successful in the long run, you need to start saving and investing early in life. By putting money aside and investing in your future on a regular basis, you can grow your wealth, reach your financial goals, and protect yourself from bad luck. This guide will show you how important it is to save money and invest, as well as give you tips on how to get into these habits.

1. Set up a fund for emergencies

An emergency fund is like a financial safety net that can help you get through things like losing your job, getting sick, or needing to make urgent repairs to your home. Try to save enough money for three to six months of living costs in a separate account that is easy to get to. This safety net gives you peace of mind and keeps you from going into debt when times are tough.

1. Save up for your goals

Once you have a good emergency fund, save for your short-term and long-term financial goals. This could mean saving up for a down payment on a house, paying for your kids' college, or planning a dream vacation. Set specific, measurable goals for each of your goals and put aside some of your money to help you reach them.

- Set up automatic savings

Consider automating your savings by setting up regular transfers from your checking account to your savings or investment accounts. This will make it easy to save money. By "paying yourself first," you make saving a priority and make sure you always put money toward your financial goals.

- Start to invest

With a solid base, you can start investing to build your wealth and make sure you have money for the future. Start small by looking into low-cost investment options like index funds, exchange-traded funds (ETFs), and low-cost mutual funds. These types of investments give you access to a wide range of markets with low costs, making them perfect for beginners.

- Spread out your investments

As you learn more about investing, try to build a diversified portfolio that matches your risk tolerance and financial goals. Diversification means spreading your investments across different types of assets (stocks, bonds, real estate, etc.) to lower risk and increase the amount of money you could make. A well-balanced portfolio protects you from changes in the market and makes sure that your investments keep growing over time.

- Learn something

Learn about different investment vehicles, strategies, and market trends so you can make smart investment decisions and get the most out of your money. This could mean reading books, going to seminars, or following reliable sources of financial news. Keep up with what's going on in the market and keep learning as your investing experience grows.

- Review and change your plan for investing

Review your investment portfolio often to make sure it still fits with your financial goals and how much risk you are willing to take. As things change in your life, you may need to change your investment plan to match your new priorities. This could mean rebalancing your investments, looking for new ways to invest, or changing your focus to other financial goals.

CHAPTER 1.E

I t's important to know what your personal financial values are so you can make decisions that are in line with your overall goals and aspirations. These values guide you through different financial situations and help you decide how to spend your money. In this guide, we'll talk about how to figure out what your financial values are and how to live by them.

- Think about what you've done in your life

Start by thinking about the things you've done in your life, especially those that have to do with money. Think about how your upbringing, culture, and personal experiences have affected the way you feel about money. Think about any money successes, problems, or lessons you've learned and how they've changed the way you think about money.

- Figure out your priorities

Next, think about what's most important to you when it comes to money. This could mean taking care of your family, retiring comfortably, giving to charity, or becoming financially independent. If you know what your priorities are, you can use your time and money on the things that are most important to you.

- Define Your Core Values

Set your core financial values by thinking about what's most important to you. Some of these values might be safety, freedom, kindness, stability, or growth. Be honest with yourself and think about which values you hold most dear. Remember that your financial values are unique to you and may be different from those of your friends, family, or peers.

- Match your goals with what you care about

Once you know what your financial values are, make sure your financial goals are in line with them. For example, if being financially independent is a core value, your goals could include paying off debt, building passive income streams, or investing in your education to increase your earning potential. By making goals that fit with your values, you'll be more likely to stay motivated and committed to achieving them.

- Choose based on what you want

Make decisions about your money that reflect your priorities and beliefs and are based on what you value. This could mean choosing to pay off your debts first instead of buying things you don't need, giving money to good causes, or investing in businesses that align with your values. By making financial decisions that are in line with your values, you'll be happier and more satisfied with your financial journey.

- Communicate Your Values

Talk to your other half, family, or close friends about how you feel about money. When you talk openly about your values, you can help each other understand and support each other's beliefs. This makes it easier to work together toward shared financial goals or get through financial problems.

- Regularly Reevaluate Your Values

Lastly, realize that your values about money may change over time as your life changes and your priorities shift. Check in on your values often and make changes to your financial goals and decisions based on what you find. This will help you keep your financial decisions in line with your overall goals for your life.

CHAPTER 2

It can be hard for young people to figure out how to handle their own money. Income and taxes are two of the most important things to learn about. In this guide, we'll go into more detail about different ways to make money, the difference between gross and net income, paying taxes in a responsible way, and how important tax deductions and credits are.

Sources of Money

As a young adult, it's important to know about all the different ways you can make money. Some popular ways to make money are:

a. Salary: A set amount of money paid to an employee on a regular basis. It is usually given as a yearly amount.

b. Wages: Payment is based on the number of hours done, and each hour is paid at an agreed-upon rate.

c. Self-Employment Income: Money made by freelancing, contracting, or running a small business.

d. Tips and commissions: Extra money that people who work in sales or service get from customers' tips or commissions on sales.

e. Investment Income: This includes dividends, interest, and capital gains from financial assets.

f. Rental Income: Money that comes from renting out a house or flat.

Net Income vs. Gross Income

For budgeting and financial planning, it's important to know the difference between gross and net money. Gross income is the amount of money made before taxes or deductions are taken out. Net income is the amount of money left over after taxes and deductions are taken out. To keep track of your money well, your budget needs to be based on your net income, which is the amount you can spend and save.

Responsible Tax Filing

Filing taxes correctly and on time is an important part of managing money for young adults. To do your taxes the right way:

a. Report all types of income: Make sure you report all the money you made during the tax year.

b. Use any relevant tax deductions and credits: Learn about the tax deductions and credits that can help you pay less in taxes.

c. Pay any taxes you owe: If you owe taxes, make sure to pay them by the deadline to avoid fees and interest.

d. Get help from a professional if you need to: If you're not sure about your tax situation, you might want to talk to a tax pro or use tax tools to make sure you're doing things right.

Tax Breaks and Tax Credits

Tax exemptions and tax credits are important ways to lower your tax bill. Credits directly lower the amount of tax you owe, while deductions lower the amount of your money that is taxed. Some of the most common tax breaks and credits for young adults are:

a. Registered Retirement Savings Plans (RRSP): An RRSP is an account that Canadian residents can use to save for retirement. Contributions to an RRSP are tax-deductible, which means they lower the amount of your money that is subject to tax. The money in an RRSP grows tax-free until you take it out, which is usually when you retire, and your income is likely to be lower. At that time, you would pay less tax on the money.

b. Registered Education Savings Plans (RESP): An RESP is a tax-advantaged account that helps Canadian residents save for their children's post-secondary schooling. Even though you can't get a tax break for the money you put into a RESP, the money you make on your investments grows tax-free. When money is taken out to pay for school, it is taxed at the student's rate, which is usually cheaper than the contributor's rate.

c. Deduction for student loan interest: This lets you write off the interest you pay on certain student loans.

d. American Opportunity Tax Credit: Gives eligible students a tax credit for qualified school costs.

e. Earned Income Tax Credit: This is a credit for people and families with low to middle incomes who work and pay taxes.

By understanding and using these tax deductions and credits, young people can get the most money out of their money and pay the least amount of taxes. It's important to know about the tax breaks that are offered in your country and how they affect your particular finances.

I'm not a tax expert. Please consult a tax expert in your area.

Keeping your financial paperwork in order

Keeping your financial paperwork in order is important if you want to file your taxes easily and with as few mistakes as possible. To stay in order:

a. Make a filing system: Either physically or digitally, set up a way to organize your financial papers.

b. Keep track of your income and expenses: Keep track of all sources of income, tax-deductible expenses, and documents connected to taxes.

c. Keep your records up to date: Look over and update your financial records throughout the year to avoid stressing out at the last minute when tax time comes around.

CHAPTER 3

M anaging your money as a young adult requires that you know how important it is to save money. You can get financial stability and peace of mind by setting aside money for both short-term goals, like vacations or emergency costs, and long-term goals, like retirement or buying a home. This part goes into detail about the different ways to save, how compound interest works, and how to get the most out of your savings over time.

The Benefits of Saving Money

Saving money can help you reach your financial goals, which is one of its most important benefits. Putting money away on a regular basis lets you work towards both short-term goals and long-term goals. For example, saving for short-term goals, like paying for a trip, lets you have memorable experiences and well-deserved breaks without going into debt. These things can make your life better and give you memories that will last a long time.

Aside from helping you reach short-term goals, saving money is also a key part of reaching long-term goals, like having a good retirement.

By saving and investing wisely over time, you can protect your financial future and make sure you can live the way you want after you stop working. This long-term financial planning can help you avoid problems in your golden years and give you the freedom to follow your interests and passions without worrying about money.

Also, saving money helps you reach other important goals, like buying a house or having a family. A solid savings plan can give you the money you need to reach these goals and build the life you want for yourself and your family.

In the end, saving money helps you build the life you want by giving you the money you need to reach your short-term and long-term goals. By putting money away on a regular basis, you invest in your future and give yourself access to new chances and experiences that can make your life better as a whole.

Goal-setting for the Short and Long Term

Before you start saving, it's important to figure out what your short-term and long-term goals are. If you know what you're working towards, you'll be better able to make a plan that will help you reach your goals.

Most short-term goals involve spending money you plan to spend in the next few years. You could save up for a much-needed trip, save up for a down payment on a car, or start an emergency fund to protect yourself from unexpected financial problems. By setting short-term goals, you can feel good when you reach these targets, which can encourage you to keep saving for your long-term goals.

Long-term goals, on the other hand, are money goals that may take years or even decades to reach. Some of these goals are to have a good retirement, buy a home, or pay for a child's college education. Long-term goals require you to save more money and often involve using investments in a smart way to help your money grow over time.

Once your short-term and long-term goals are clear, you can make a plan to reach them. This could mean setting aside a certain amount of your income for each goal, using different ways to save money, and checking in on your progress often to make sure you stay on track. If you have a plan, you can stay focused on your goals and make smart choices about how to use your resources most effectively.

In short, you will be more likely to save money if you write down your short-term and long-term financial goals and make a plan to reach them. This method of saving gives you more control over how you spend your money and keeps you inspired and committed to reaching your financial goals.

Your Risk Tolerance and Your Time Horizon

When deciding how to save, it's important to think about how much risk you're willing to take and how long it will take to reach each of your financial goals. These two things will have a big impact on the kinds of investments you should think about. This will help you get the best results while taking the least amount of risk.

Risk tolerance is a personal measure of how comfortable you are with the possible changes in the value of your finances. It's important to be honest about how much risk you're willing to take, because that will help you choose options that fit your comfort level. Most of the time, investments with higher potential returns are riskier than ones with lower potential yields. By matching your investments to how much risk you are willing to take, you can avoid stress and worry that could come from investments that are too risky for you.

On the other hand, time frame or time horizon is the amount of time you have to save for a specific goal. This factor has a big effect on how much risk you can take with your investments. For short-term goals, it's usually best to be more cautious (conservative), since you won't have as much time to make up for any losses. As you work towards long-term goals, you may be able to take on more risk because you have more time to ride out market changes.

When you know how much risk you are willing to take and how long you want to save for, you can choose the best way to save for your goals. For instance, if you don't like taking risks and don't have much time to save, you might choose better ways to save, like high-yield savings accounts and certificates of deposit (CDs) or Guaranteed Investment Certificates (GICs). If you are willing to take on more risk and have more time, you might think about investing in stocks, bonds, or mutual funds, which could give you better returns over time.

Therefore, figuring out how much risk you are willing to take and how long you have to save is a crucial step in making a good savings plan. If you know about these things, you can make your investments fit your level of comfort and the time you have to reach your financial goals. This personalized method will help you get the most out of your investments while minimizing risk, putting you on the path to financial success.

In the world of personal finance, there are many different ways to save money that can help you reach your short-term and long-term goals. The key is to find the right mix of accounts and investments that maximizes your earnings while minimizing risk. Using these ways to save money and understanding how compound interest works can have a big effect on your general financial growth.

Exploring Savings Vehicles

In the world of personal finance, there are many different ways to save money that can help you reach your short-term and long-term goals. The key is to find the right mix of accounts and investments that maximizes your earnings while minimizing risk. Using these ways to save money and understanding how compound interest works can have a big effect on your general financial growth.

GICs, CDs, money market accounts, and high-yield savings accounts are all popular choices for conservative investors who want a safe place to put their money and earn some interest at the same time. But if you want to spread your investments out more and possibly make more money, you may want to look into bonds, stocks, mutual funds, exchange-traded funds (ETFs), and retirement accounts.

Bonds are debt securities that governments or companies put out to raise money. When you buy a bond, you're basically giving the issuer a loan. The issuer agrees to pay you interest payments on a regular basis and give you back the principal when the bond matures. Bonds can be a relatively safe way to invest because they offer predictable profits and less risk than stocks in general.

Stocks are parts of a company that can be bought and sold. As an investor, you could make money from capital gains if the stock's value goes up, and you could also get money from dividends. But stocks carry a higher amount of risk than other investments because their value can change a lot depending on how the market is doing.

Mutual funds are a way to invest in a variety of stocks, bonds, and other assets by pooling money together. Professional fund managers are in charge of running these funds. They try to meet the owners' investment goals on their behalf. Mutual funds can help you spread your risk and give you the chance to make more money, but they may also have management fees and other costs.

Exchange-traded funds (ETFs) are like mutual funds in that they hold a variety of investments. ETFs, on the other hand, can be bought and sold on a market like stocks, which gives them more flexibility and usually lower fees than mutual funds. ETFs can be a good choice for people who want to diversify their investments and trade throughout the day.

It's important to think about tax-advantaged accounts like Roth Individual Retirement Accounts (Roth IRAs) in the United States and Tax-Free Savings Accounts (TFSAs) in Canada when you're handling your money and looking for ways to save. Both accounts have their own perks that can help you make the most of your savings and investments and pay the least amount of tax.

In the United States, a Roth IRA is a tax-advantaged retirement savings account that lets your money grow tax-free. Donations are made with money that has already been taxed, so you don't get a tax break right away for the amount you give. However the gains in the account grow tax-free, and qualified withdrawals during retirement are also tax-free. Roth IRAs can hold different kinds of investments, like stocks, bonds, mutual funds, and exchange-traded funds (ETFs). This gives you the chance to spread your portfolio and make sure that your investments match your risk tolerance and financial goals.

In the same way, a Tax-Free Savings Account (TFSA) in Canada is a flexible and tax-efficient way to save money that lets you save and spend for both short-term and long-term goals. Contributions to a TFSA are also made with money that has already been taxed, and the account's interest, earnings, and capital gains are not taxed. The main benefit of a TFSA is that it grows tax-free, and you can take money out tax-free at any time for any reason. This makes it a flexible way to manage your savings.

Depending on where you live, if you use both Roth IRAs and TFSAs in your financial plan, you can take advantage of the tax-free growth these accounts offer and work more efficiently toward your financial goals. Using these tax-advantaged accounts along with other ways to save, like high-yield savings accounts, certificates of deposit (CDs), and money market accounts, can help you make a well-rounded and effective savings plan that fits your wants and goals.

Lastly, retirement plans like 401(k)s, IRAs, and RRSPs can help you save for retirement by giving you tax breaks. These accounts let you invest in stocks, bonds, and mutual funds, among other things, while getting tax breaks that can make compound interest work better over time.

The Magic of Compound Interest

Compound interest is one of the most important things you can do with your money. This makes it possible for your savings to grow faster and faster over time, because the interest you earn is re-invested and makes you more money. The longer you save and invest, the more effect compound interest has on your money. This helps you reach your financial goals faster and more efficiently.

When you want to use the power of compound interest, you must start early. If you start saving and investing right away, your money will have more time to grow and gain from compounding. The snowball effect of compound interest means that even small, regular payments can add up to a lot of money over time.

Consistency is also a key part of getting the most out of compound interest. By putting money into your savings and investments daily, you build momentum and speed up the process of getting rich. Whether you put money away every month or every two weeks, having a plan can help you stay on track and take advantage of the power of growth.

Lastly, to get the most out of compound interest, it's important to choose savings vehicles with competitive interest rates. Make sure to compare the rates and terms of different accounts and investments, such as high-yield savings accounts, CDs, and money market accounts. If you choose choices with higher rates, your savings will grow faster, thanks to the power of compound interest.

Strategies for Maximizing Savings Growth

To get the most out of your money, it's important to have a clear plan. Start by putting your money goals in order of importance. Figure out which goals are most important to you and use your money to reach those goals. This will help you focus on what's most important and get the most out of the money you've worked hard for.

Make sure you have money set aside for emergencies before you move on to other financial goals. This fund should have enough money to cover living costs for three to six months. This gives you a safety net in case something unexpected happens, like losing your job or getting sick. Having this cushion will keep you from going into debt and help you stick to your financial plan even when things get tough.

Automating your savings is another good way to get the most out of your money. Set up automatic transfers from your checking account to your savings or investment accounts. This will help you reach your financial goals more frequently. If you make saving a natural part of your daily life, you're more likely to stick to your plan and reach your goals.

It's also important to look at your plan often and make changes to it. Keep track of how far you are from your goals and make changes to your money plan as needed. This could mean increasing the amount you save, moving money around, or changing the way you spend. Checking in on a regular basis will help you stay on track and adjust your plan if your finances or goals change.

Last, don't be afraid to ask for help from a professional. If you're not sure how to save or need help coming up with a plan, you might want to talk to a financial adviser for advice that fits your specific situation. A professional can help you figure out how to handle your personal finances and make sure you're making decisions that are well-informed and in line with your goals.

By using these tactics and realizing how important it is to save money for both short-term and long-term goals, you can build a strong financial base and work toward your financial goals.

CHAPTER 4

M any young people have debt, whether it's from student loans, credit card balances, or car loans. To do a good job of handling your money, you need to know how debt and credit work. In this chapter, we'll talk about the differences between good and bad debt, how to handle both kinds, and how to build and keep good credit. We'll also talk about ways to pay off debt, like the debt snowball method and the debt avalanche method.

Good Debt Vs Bad Debt

It's important to know the difference between good and bad debt if you want to make smart decisions about borrowing money. As the name suggests, good debt can help you grow your money and keep it stable. When you get good debt, you're putting money into your future. For example, student loans can help you go to college, which can lead to a higher income and better job prospects. With a mortgage, you can buy a home, which is usually a good long-term investment because home prices tend to go up over time. When used wisely, small business loans can help you start or grow a business, which will bring in money and make you rich.

On the other hand, bad debt usually comes from buying things or taking out loans that don't help your long-term financial health. Everyday spending can quickly add up on your credit card balance, especially if you don't pay it off in full every month. Payday loans and other high-interest loans can trap you in a circle of debt because the interest rates and fees are so high. Borrowing to buy assets that lose value quickly, like a new car with a high-interest loan, is also called bad debt, since the value of the asset drops quickly while you're still paying off the loan.

The best way to handle debt is to know the difference between good and bad debt and to think carefully about how your borrowing choices will affect you in the long run. You can set yourself up for a more stable financial future by focusing on good debt that helps you reach your financial goals and avoiding bad debt that can slow you down.

Debt Management

Managing your debt is an important part of keeping your finances in good shape. The first step in getting control of your debt is to understand the terms and conditions of each loan and credit deal you have. Check each remaining balance's interest rate, minimum payment amount, and length of time to pay it off. Having this information will give you the power to make smart decisions about how to deal with your debt and use your money wisely.

Once you have a clear picture of all your outstanding bills, make a full list with all the important information. This will let you make a plan for paying back the loan that fits your budget and helps you reach your financial goals. When making a plan to pay off debt, it's usually best to pay off the debt with the highest interest rate first, since it will cost you the most in the long run. This is what is known as the "Debt

Avalanche Method."

But some people may be more motivated to start by paying off smaller bills first, no matter how much the interest is. This method, called the "debt snowball method," has you make the minimum payments on all of your debts and put any extra money toward the one with the smallest amount. When the smallest debt is paid off, the money that was going toward it is moved to the next smallest debt. This is called the "snowball effect." This can give you a sense of achievement and encourage you to stick to your plan for paying off your debt.

Along with picking a plan that fits your tastes and financial goals, it's important to keep track of your progress and make changes as needed. Check your balances, interest rates, and payment records on a regular basis to make sure you're making steady progress toward getting out of debt. If your money situation changes, you should be ready to change your plan. By staying busy and on top of your debt management, you'll be better able to deal with problems and, in the end, get out of debt.

Understanding Credit Scores and Building Good Credit

A credit score is an important part of your financial picture. It is a number that shows how creditworthy you are. Credit scores are often used by lenders, landlords, and even jobs to figure out how reliable and responsible you are with money. If you have a good credit score, you can get better loan terms, lower interest rates, and more chances in many areas of your life.

Learning what goes into your credit score is the first step to building and keeping good credit. Here are some of the most important ones:

- Payment history: A big part of your credit score is how well you have paid your bills on time in the past. Making payments on time or before the due date shows that you can be trusted and are serious about meeting your financial responsibilities.

- Credit utilization ratio: This is how much of your available credit you are using right now. For a good credit score, it's usually best to use less than 30% of your available credit. This means that if your credit card has a limit of $10,000, you should try to keep the amount below $3,000.

- Length of credit history: Your credit score will be higher if you have been using credit for a long time. A longer history tells possible lenders more about how you handle debt and how often you borrow.

- Credit types: Having a variety of credit accounts, like credit cards, mortgages, and monthly loans, can help your credit score. It shows that you can handle different kinds of debt in a responsible way.

- New credit inquiries: Trying to get new credit too often can hurt your credit score. Every time you apply, a hard inquiry is made, which can briefly lower your score. Don't fill out too many credit forms if you don't want to hurt your credit score.

By paying attention to these things and managing your credit well, you can build and keep a good credit score. Check your credit records from the three major credit bureaus, Experian, Equifax, and TransUnion, on a regular basis to make sure the information is correct and to spot any signs of fraud or identity theft. By keeping an eye on your credit and taking action, you will be well on your way to getting and keeping good credit.

Paying Off Debt: The Debt Snowball and Debt Avalanche Methods

Finding the best way to pay off debt is important if you want to be financially free. The debt snowball method and the debt avalanche method are two famous ways to deal with debt. Each method has its own advantages, and the one you choose will rely on your financial goals and personal preferences.

The debt snowball method is based on paying off your debts from the smallest amount to the largest balance, no matter how much interest you are paying. This method gives you a sense of accomplishment because you can see how quickly you're getting rid of smaller debts. This can keep you inspired to keep paying off your other debts. As you pay off one debt, the money you used to pay it off gets "snowballed" into the next payment, making it easier to pay off the next debt.

The debt avalanche method, on the other hand, tells you to pay off the bills with the highest interest rates first. This method can save you money in the long run because you'll pay off the bills with the highest interest rates first. To use the debt avalanche method, you'll make minimum payments on all of your bills and put any extra money toward the debt with the highest interest rate. Once that debt is paid off, you'll move on to the next debt with the biggest interest rate, and so on, until you have no more debt.

In the end, you should choose between the debt snowball and debt avalanche methods based on your own financial goals and how you keep yourself inspired. Some people might like how the debt snowball method gives them quick wins, while others might like how the debt slide method helps them save money over time. No matter what method you choose, the most important thing is to stay steady and committed to paying off your debt and getting out of debt.

To close Chapter 4, if you want to be good with your money as a young adult, you need to deal with debt and build credit. The first step toward making smart choices about borrowing money is to understand the differences between good debt and bad debt. Knowing the possible pros and cons of different kinds of debt can help you make decisions that are good for your long-term financial health.

Creating a plan for paying off debt is an important part of handling debt well. By making a plan that fits with your budget and financial goals, you can slowly work toward paying off your debt and freeing up money for other things. Sticking to a regular payback plan not only helps you pay off your debts, but it also teaches you good money habits that will serve you well for the rest of your life.

Keeping good credit is another important part of managing money. When you have good credit, you can get better loan terms, lower interest rates, and even better job chances. By paying your bills on time, keeping your credit card balances low, and not applying for credit when you don't need to, you can build and keep a good credit past that will help you for years to come.

It's important to be proactive, persistent, and patient as you work toward financial freedom. Financial success doesn't happen fast; it comes from working hard and making good decisions over time. By getting rid of debt, building credit, and keeping an eye on the long run, you can set yourself up for a stable financial future and the freedom that comes with being financially independent.

CHAPTER 5

Young people may find it hard to understand the world of investing, but it's an important part of building long-term wealth and achieving financial security. In this chapter, we'll talk about the different ways to invest, why diversification is important, and how to choose an investment plan that fits your goals and level of risk tolerance.

Stocks, Bonds and Mutual Funds

Stocks let buyers own a piece of a company, which can lead to capital gains if the value of the company goes up over time. Some stocks also give out dividends, which are regular payments of cash to owners. Even though investing in stocks can give you a chance to make a lot of money, it's important to know that they are also riskier than other types of investments. The value of stocks can change a lot depending on how the market is doing, how well the company is doing, and other things.

On the other hand, bonds are safer investments that involve giving money to states or businesses. In exchange for the loan, the bond issuer agrees to pay the investor a fixed rate of interest over a set period of time. When the bond hits its maturity date, the investor is paid back the principal amount. Bonds can give you a steady stream of money, and most people think they are less risky than stocks. They usually give smaller returns, though.

Mutual funds are a unique mix of stocks and bonds that allow buyers to take advantage of the growth potential of stocks while keeping some of the stability of bonds. Mutual funds can offer diversification and skilled management because they pool the money of many investors. This can be especially helpful for people who are new to investing. Mutual funds can put their money into stocks, bonds, real estate, and other assets with different levels of risk and possible returns.

If you know a lot about these different ways to invest, you'll be able to make better decisions about your investment plan. When deciding which investments are right for you, it's important to think about your financial goals, how comfortable you are with risk, and how long you have to spend. This information will give you a solid base for making a portfolio of investments that is diverse and does well.

Diversification

Diversification is called the "golden rule" of trading for a good reason. Spreading your money out over a number of different investments and industries is a way to "hedge your bets." This strategy helps protect your investment portfolio from the ups and downs of the market because the performance of one asset class or area doesn't affect the performance of your entire portfolio as a whole. In other words, if one item in your portfolio doesn't do well, the others may still do well, making up for any losses.

Your money goals are a big factor in figuring out how diversified your investment portfolio should be. If you're saving for a short-term goal, like a down payment on a house or a trip coming up, you might want to spend more conservatively by putting your money into bonds or money market accounts, which are less likely to go up or down. On the other hand, if you're saving for a long-term goal, like retirement or a child's college education, you might be more willing to invest in risky things, like stocks or real estate, that could pay off in the long run.

When you diversify your money, you should also think about how willing you are to take risks. some investors are willing to take on more risk in order to make more money, while others prefer to be more cautious in order to keep their money safe. Your risk tolerance will determine what kinds of assets you put in your portfolio and how much you spend in each.

Lastly, the amount of diversification you should aim for depends on how long you plan to keep your money in the market. Most of the time, investors with a longer time frame can take on more risk because they have more time to recover from possible losses. As you get closer to your investment goals, you may want to slowly move your portfolio toward safer options to keep your gains and lower your risk.

Time Horizon and Risk Tolerance

Your level of comfort with risk and your investment goals are like a road map that shows you where to spend. Just like a road map helps you get where you want to go, knowing how much risk you are willing to take and what you want to achieve with your investments will help you make a plan that works for you. It's important to remember that everyone's risk tolerance and personal investment goals are different, so there's no one way to invest that works for everyone.

Risk tolerance is affected by many things, like your age, your finances, and how you've handled money in the past. Younger investors who have more time to meet their goals may be more willing to take on more risk because they have more time to get back on their feet if they lose money. On the other hand, investors who are getting close to retirement or who have a shorter time horizon may choose a more conservative strategy that puts capital protection ahead of aggressive returns.

As a young adult, it's important to set SMART (specific, measurable, realistic, relevant, and time-bound) goals for your investments. By setting clear goals, you'll be able to make better investment choices and keep your eye on your financial goals. For example, if you want to save for a down payment on a house or build up an emergency fund, you'll probably choose investments that can grow enough over time while still giving you a level of safety that matches your risk tolerance.

When deciding between different investment choices, you should think about the risks and rewards that come with each one, as well as how they fit with your risk tolerance and investment goals. Some investments, like stocks and real estate, have a higher chance of making money, but they are also riskier. On the other hand, bonds and money market funds may be more stable, but they may not give as much money back.

Understanding how long you plan to keep your investments is important for figuring out how diversified your portfolio should be. With a longer time span, investors can take on more risk because they have more time to get back to even if they lose money. When you're young and just beginning to invest, you have time on your side. This gives you the chance to try out a wider range of investments, including ones that are riskier but could pay off more in the long run.

As you get closer to your investment goals, it's a good idea to check in on your risk tolerance and time frame. This evaluation will help you make the right changes to your business plan. For example, as you get closer to the end of your time frame, you may want to slowly move your portfolio toward safer investments, like bonds or stocks that pay dividends. This change can help you keep the money you've made over the years and lower the chance that you'll lose a lot of money right before you need the money.

In the end, young adults, like you, need to know how diversification, risk tolerance, and the length of time you plan to spend affect your investment strategy. By keeping these things in mind and making changes to your portfolio as needed, you can handle the market's ups and downs with more confidence and work toward a safe financial future.

Tax-Advantaged Accounts

Young adults who want to get the most out of their investments can use tax-advantaged accounts to do so. By using these accounts, you could save thousands of dollars in taxes over the life of your investment career. Each account type has its own features and perks, so it's important to know what they are so you can use them to their fullest.

A Tax-Free Savings Account, or TFSA, lets you put money in after you've already paid taxes on it. This means that the money you're saving has already been taxed. Both the growth of a TFSA and the money you take out of it are tax-free, which makes it a great choice for both short-term and long-term savings goals.

Like TFSAs, Roth IRAs let you put in money that you've already paid taxes on, and your investments grow tax-free. But Roth IRAs are meant for saving for retirement and have rules about how much you can put in and when you can take money out.

On the other hand, RRSPs and 401(k)s are accounts that don't have to pay taxes right away. You put money into these accounts before you pay taxes, so you get a tax break in the year you put money in. The savings in these accounts grow tax-free, but when you take the money out in retirement, you'll have to pay taxes on it.

When you're a young adult, it's important to think about both your current and future tax position when deciding which tax-advantaged accounts to focus on. For example, if you think your tax bracket will be higher in the future, a Roth IRA or TFSA may be better because you won't have to pay taxes on withdrawals when you leave. If you think your tax bracket will be lower when you retire, on the other hand, a 401(k) or RRSP may be a better choice.

By using tax-advantaged accounts as part of your investment plan, you may be able to increase your long-term gains and move closer to your financial goals. Talk to a financial adviser or tax expert to make sure you're making the best choices for your specific situation.

Maximize Your Contribution

Contributing as much as possible to all tax-advantaged accounts can be a great way for young adults to get the most out of their money. Depending on your present and future tax situation, you may be able to use the different account types to get both tax-free growth and tax-deferred savings.

To get the most out of all kinds of accounts, it's important to know how much you can put into each one. Make sure to check these limits often, because they may change from one year to the next. By putting the most you can into each account, you can get the most out of the tax benefits and help your money grow faster.

Keep in mind that maxing out your contributions to multiple tax-advantaged accounts may require a big chunk of your money. As a young adult, it's important to find a good mix between investing in these accounts and other financial goals, like building an emergency fund, paying off high-interest debt, or saving for a down payment on a house.

Also, it's important to keep a diversified investment portfolio across all of your accounts, taking into account your general financial goals, how comfortable you are with risk, and how long you plan to invest. Depending on the tax benefits and your own financial position, this may mean putting different types of assets or investment vehicles in each account.

In a nutshell, young people who want to get the most out of their money can do well to put as much as they can into all tax-advantaged accounts. By making the most of the tax benefits these accounts offer and keeping a varied portfolio of investments, you can reach your financial goals more quickly. But before you commit to this strategy, you should think about your general financial situation and priorities and talk to a financial advisor to make sure it's the right one for you.

CHAPTER 6

As a young adult, it's important to know that insurance is a good way to protect your finances. In this chapter, we'll talk about different kinds of insurance you might want to think about and give you tips on how to choose the right coverage for your needs. We'll also talk about how important it is to look over and update your insurance plans regularly.

Health Insurance

When it comes to paying for medical bills, health insurance is a very important financial safety net. Unexpected health problems can happen at any time, and if you don't have the right coverage, the costs can be too much to handle. As you look at your health insurance choices, there are a few key things you should think about.

The payments you make each month to keep your insurance benefits are called premiums. When comparing plans, it's important to think about both how much the premiums cost and how much support they give. Keep in mind that bigger deductibles or out-of-pocket costs may come with lower premiums.

Deductibles are the amount you have to pay out of pocket for medical bills before your insurance starts to pay for them. Higher deductibles usually mean lower monthly rates, but you may have to pay more up front for medical care if you need it.

Copayments are set fees you pay for certain healthcare services, like doctor visits or prescriptions. Depending on the service and the insurance plan you choose, these fees can be different.

Out-of-pocket maximums set a limit on how much you'll have to pay for health care in a given year. Once you hit this limit, your insurance will pay for all of your remaining medical costs for the year. It's important to think about this limit when choosing a plan to make sure you can pay for any health care costs that might come up.

Also, it's important to look at the network of doctors and hospitals that are part of the plan. Some insurance plans have very tight rules about which doctors or hospitals you can go to, while others give you more freedom. Make sure the plan you choose covers the doctors or hospitals you like or need for your health.

Extra perks, like coverage for your teeth or eyes, can also affect your choice of health insurance plan. Some policies may not cover these perks, so it's important to think about what you need and check if they are included.

Finally, if you are able to remain under your parents' health insurance, do so. This is a financial savvy move. This alternative can help you keep your coverage while reducing the amount you pay on your premiums.

Auto Insurance

Auto insurance is very important because it protects you and your car from financial losses that could be caused by accidents, theft, and other unplanned events. It's important to carefully study and choose an auto insurance policy that fits your needs and budget. You can find the best deal on insurance by comparing rates and coverage choices from different companies.

When looking at car insurance policies, keep in mind that higher deductibles often mean lower monthly premiums, but you'll have to be ready to pay more of the repair costs if you get into an accident. Also, it's important to know about the different types of coverage, like comprehensive, collision, and uninsured/underinsured motorist coverage, so you can decide what kind of security you need.

It's also a good idea to look over your car insurance policy from time to time to make sure it still fits your needs. Changes in your life, like moving to a new area or buying a new car, may require you to make changes to your insurance. By staying informed and taking charge of your car insurance, you can make sure you're safe on the road and keep your costs down.

Renter's Insurance

Renters insurance gives people and families who live in rental homes peace of mind by protecting their belongings and giving them important liability protection. When choosing a renter's insurance policy, it's important to take a complete inventory of your things so you can get a good idea of how much they're worth. This will help you figure out how much coverage you need and make sure you are well protected in case of a loss. It's important to know the difference between actual cash worth and replacement cost coverage, in addition to the coverage limits. Actual cash value policies pay you the reduced value of your things, while replacement cost policies give you the money you need to replace your things with new ones that are the same or similar. Even though the rates for replacement cost coverage may be higher, it can help you save more money in the long run.

Lastly, it's important to check and update your renter's insurance policy on a regular basis to account for any big changes in your living situation or the value of your things. For example, you may need to change your coverage if you buy new, high-value items or if you move to a different rental home. Staying proactive and aware of your renter's insurance can help make sure you are always protected and ready for the unexpected.

Life Insurance

Life insurance can play a critical role in protecting your family's financial future, especially if you are the main breadwinner or have significant debts. When exploring life insurance choices, it's important to determine how much coverage you need by taking into account factors such as your current income, outstanding debts, and the financial needs of your dependents.

Term Insurance

Term life insurance is often the most cost-effective choice for young adults, as it provides coverage for a specific term, usually 10, 20, or 30 years. This type of policy is intended to provide financial protection during the years when your dependents may be most reliant on your income. Premiums for term life insurance plans tend to be lower than those for permanent life insurance, making it an attractive choice for individuals on a budget or those who only need coverage for a particular period.

When shopping for a term life insurance policy, it's essential to compare quotes from various insurance providers to find the best rates and coverage options. Additionally, consider the financial strength and reputation of the insurer to ensure that they will be able to meet their obligations in the event of a claim.

Permanent Life Insurance

For young adults who want more than a term policy, there are permanent life insurance choices like whole life, universal life, and variable life insurance. As long as you pay your premiums, these plans cover you for your whole life, and they often have a cash value that can grow over time.

Whole life insurance has set premiums, a guaranteed death benefit, and a cash value that grows at a fixed rate of interest. Universal life insurance gives you more freedom because you can change your premium payments and death benefit, but only within certain boundaries. In a universal life insurance, the cash value is tied to a certain interest rate, which can change over time. Variable life insurance plans let you invest the cash value in different ways, like stocks and bonds. This gives you the chance to make more money, but also puts you at a higher level of risk.

Permanent life insurance plans may offer more benefits and ways to invest, but the premiums are usually higher than those for term life insurance. Before making a choice, young adults should carefully consider the costs and benefits of these policies in light of their current financial situation and future goals.

I just want to add a little disclaimer here; I'm not an insurance agent or an expert in insurance. Therefore, when making choices about insurance, I truly recommend for you to talk to someone who knows a lot about the subject. Insurance agents know a lot about the different policies, coverage choices, and possible discounts that are available to you. They can figure out what you need and help you find the best insurance products for you, taking into account things like your income, how you live, and any special needs you may have. By working closely with an insurance expert, you'll pick the best coverage for your wants and protect your financial well-being.

Finding Affordable Policies

Don't be afraid to deal with insurance companies when you're looking for cheap plans. If a company knows you are looking at more than one choice, they may be willing to give you a better deal. Tell them if you've gotten a better offer from another company, because they might be ready to match or beat it to get your business.

Another way to lower your insurance rates is to raise your deductible, which is the amount you pay out of pocket before the insurance coverage kicks in. This will cost you more if you make a claim, but it can make your monthly fees a lot less. Just make sure you have enough money saved up to pay the higher cost if you need to.

It's also important to review and change your insurance coverage every so often to make sure it fits your wants and changes in life. For example, if the value of your personal items goes up or if you buy something new, you may need to change the coverage on your renters or homeowners insurance. In the same way, your life insurance needs may change as your family grows or as your financial responsibilities change.

By being cautious and keeping an eye on your insurance coverage, you can make sure that you are not only getting enough protection but also the best rates for your needs. Remember that the best way to find cheap insurance plans is to be thorough, knowledgeable, and active in your search.

Reviewing and Updating Coverage

By reviewing your insurance coverage on a regular basis, you can also find any holes or overlaps in your coverage. This will help you avoid paying for coverage you don't need or not having enough coverage in some places. Also, it's a good idea to learn about any insurance exclusions so that you can make sure you have the right coverage for your needs.

Reviewing your insurance benefits on a regular basis also gives you the chance to look at your deductibles again. As your finances change, you may be able to afford a bigger deductible, which can lower the cost of your premiums. On the other hand, if you recently lost money or your risk tolerance has changed, you might want to lower your deductible and pay a slightly higher rate for a little more peace of mind.

Lastly, it's important to let your insurance company know about any big changes in your life or personal information. Keeping your insurance company up-to-date will help make sure that your coverage is still current and correct, giving you the protection you need as you move through life's different stages.

CHAPTER 7

As a young adult, you need to learn how to handle your money. This is a skill that will help you for the rest of your life. One of the most important parts of managing money is learning how to spend money wisely. In this chapter, we'll talk about how to tell the difference between what you want and what you need, make a budget and stick to it, and use credit cards in a smart way. Also, we'll talk about some ways to shop that can help you save money without giving up the things you love.

How to Tell the Difference Between Wants and Needs

To be financially successful, you need to learn how to tell the difference between what you want and what you need. When you're out and about, it's easy to be tempted by shiny new tools, mouth-watering meals, or that killer pair of shoes. But like a Jedi who has mastered the Force, you have to learn to control your emotions and spend money wisely.

Our lives are built on our needs. We eat, wear clothes, live in a safe place, and stay healthy because of these things. Make sure that your needs are met first when you spend your hard-earned money. It's like putting on your own breathing mask before helping others: you can't get your finances in order until you've taken care of the basics.

Let's talk about what we want next. We all have them, and that's not a bad thing. After all, life is for having fun! But it's important to think about what you want and how it fits into your money plan as a whole. By thinking about what you want and how much money you have, you can make better spending choices that won't throw off your financial goals.

So, how do you find a good mix between what you want and what you need? Start by taking a close look at how you spend your money. Do you always have what you need, or do you cut back on necessities to pay for your latest shopping trip? If your wants are taking over, it's time to take a step back and think about what's really important.

When you have to spend money, stop and ask yourself, "Is this something I want or something I need?" Give yourself time to think about how this buy fits in with your other financial goals and priorities. And don't forget that it's okay to treat yourself once in a while, as long as you're taking care of your needs first.

If you can tell the difference between what you want and what you need, you'll be better able to make smart decisions about your money. Remember, young padawan, that you have the power to make smart spending choices. If you use that power, you'll be well on your way to getting your finances in order.

Creating and Sticking to a Budget

Budgeting is like following a financial map that helps you reach your goals and stays on track. By making a budget, you take charge of your money instead of letting it take charge of you. So let's learn more about planning and how to make it work for you.

Start budgeting by keeping track of your money and spending for a couple of months. This will show you where your money is going and help you find any trends in how you spend it. Once you know how much money is coming in and going out, it's time to divide your spending into different categories, such as housing, food, transportation, and fun. Think of these groups as the bricks that make up your money life.

Now that you know where your money is going, you need to set reasonable limits for each category based on your financial goals. Make sure you're being honest with yourself and that you can reach these goals. There's no point in setting yourself up to fail. Once you've decided how much you can spend, make a promise to stick to those bounds.

Now, you may be wondering how to hold yourself responsible and make sure you stick to your budget. This is where tools for planning come in. You could use an app or calendar to keep track of your spending in real time. These tools can help you find places where you're spending too much and make the necessary changes. Plus, they remind you of your money goals all the time, keeping you motivated and on track.

Lastly, understand that your budget is a document that changes over time. There are always surprises in life, and your finances may change over time. By reviewing and updating your budget often, you can make sure it stays a useful tool for handling your money. So, use planning to your advantage and take control of your money.

Using Credit Cards Responsibly

Responsible credit card use can sometimes feel like walking a tightrope, but with a little bit of self-control and planning, you'll be able to do it like a pro. When it comes to handling your money, the key is to think of credit cards as a tool, not as a crutch to support yourself.

First, make sure that you always pay off your amount in full every month. This habit will not only keep you from falling into high-interest debt, but it will also make your credit score happy as can be. Remember that your credit score is like a report card for your finances and keeping it high can help you get loans with lower interest rates and better terms in the future.

It might be tempting to use your credit card to buy that cool new gadget, but before you do, ask yourself if you can really pay it off at the end of the month. If the answer is no, it's best to put the card away and save money instead. Spending money you don't have can be dangerous, so it's important to keep your spending under control and within your budget.

Lastly, watch how many credit cards you get. Even though the deals might sound good, having too many credit cards can make it hard to keep track of your payments and could hurt your credit score. Stick to one or two cards that fit your needs best, and you'll be well on your way to becoming a responsible credit card user.

Smart Shopping

Let me tell you something, learning how to shop smart is something you'll never regret. When you can save money without giving up the things that make life fun, it's a great feeling. So, I have a few things that I want to share with you about shopping smart.

First of all, remember that comparing costs can be your best friend. Make it a habit to do some study before you buy anything, especially big-ticket items, and things you have to pay for regularly. You'll be surprised at how much money you can save if you just shop around.

We all like to save money, so don't forget to look for sales, deals, and coupons. Trust me, there's nothing like the feeling of joy you get when you get something you want for a lot less money. And don't be afraid to buy in bulk for things you use often. It may seem like a bigger price at first, but you can save a lot of money in the long run.

Consider buying gently used things, which is another great way to save money. You might be shocked by the quality of things you can find in thrift stores or online marketplaces, and the money you save can add up quickly. In the same way, if you choose generic brands that are just as good as name brands, you can save a lot of money without losing satisfaction.

In closing, one important part of managing your money as a young adult is learning how to spend your money wisely. By putting your wants in order of importance, making a budget and sticking to it, using credit cards wisely, and shopping smart, you can take charge of your financial future and set yourself up for long-term financial success.

CHAPTER 8

As a young adult, you're definitely going to go through some big life changes that will have a big effect on your finances. Even though these things can be both exciting and hard, being ready for the money side of things can make all the difference in making the change go smoothly. In this chapter, we'll talk about some of the most common big events in life and give you tips on how to get ready for them and handle them well.

Buying a Home

As you start the process of buying a home, it's important to learn about the different types of mortgages and choose the one that works best for your finances. Fixed-rate mortgages have the same payment every month for the life of the loan, while adjustable-rate mortgages may have lower payments at first, but they go up over time. Carefully weigh the pros and cons of each choice, taking into account things like how stable your job is, how long you plan to stay in the home, and how willing you are to take risks.

Carefully weigh the pros and cons of each choice, taking into account things like how stable your job is, how long you plan to stay in the home, and how willing you are to take risks.

Getting pre-approved for a mortgage before looking for a house can help you figure out your budget and show buyers that you're a serious buyer. But pre-approval shouldn't be confused with a promise. To get the loan, you will still have to go through the full mortgage application process and meet all of the lender's standards.

Keep in mind that buying a home is more than just a money transaction; it is also an emotional one. Try not to let your feelings get in the way of your judgment as you look at possible homes. Look at each home's features, location, and possible resale value, and think about getting a professional home inspection to find any hidden problems.

Lastly, when you find the right home, be ready to compromise. Work with your real estate agent to come up with a fair offer based on the market and similar homes in the area. Be willing to give and take and remember that it's okay to walk away from a deal if it doesn't fit with your goals or money.

By taking the time to prepare financially, learn about the home-buying process, and work with knowledgeable professionals, you can confidently navigate the road to homeownership and secure a solid investment for your future.

Having Children

Aside from the money side of having kids, it's important to plan for other useful things. This means picking a pediatrician, deciding how to care for your child (e.g., daycare, nanny, or stay-at-home parent), and thinking about your family's room and safety needs as it grows. Keep in mind that you may need to change where you live, whether that means moving to a bigger home or just rearranging the space you already have to make room for a new addition.

Another important part of raising kids is showing them the value of money and getting them used to being good with money from a young age. You can help your kids learn about money by having age-appropriate conversations with them, giving them a budget, and teaching them how to save and spend wisely. As they get older, keep teaching them about things like budgeting, credit, and investing so they can make good financial choices when they're older.

Getting ready for the financial tasks of being a parent might seem hard, but if you take steps now, you can set yourself and your family up for long-term success. Focus on building a strong financial base, re-evaluating your budget and financial goals often, and teaching your children what you've learned about money. So, you can handle the challenges of having a family with confidence and help give your family a safe financial future.

Starting a Business

When thinking about how to pay for your new business, you should look at all of your choices, such as your own savings, loans, grants, or investors. Each way to get money has its pros and cons, so carefully weigh the advantages and disadvantages of each choice before deciding on one. Keep in mind that if you take on debt or get investors, you may have to take on more duties and meet higher standards.

As your business grows, you'll probably face a number of financial problems, such as keeping track of cash flow, paying taxes, and figuring out how to pay your employees. Set up a reliable bookkeeping system and stay up to date on any changes to tax laws or rules that may affect your business to stay on top of these problems. Keep an eye on your finances and change your methods as needed to keep making money and staying stable.

It's also important to have an emergency fund for your business, just like you would for your own money. This fund can be used as a safety net for unexpected costs or slow times in your business's income. This will help your business avoid financial problems.

Lastly, don't forget how important a balance between work and home is. Running a business can take up a lot of time, and it's easy to let your personal funds slip. Make your own financial health a top priority by setting aside time to look at and handle your budget, save for retirement, and invest in your future.

Starting a business can be fun and profitable, but it's important to plan ahead and keep track of your money. You can set your business up for success and build a strong foundation for a prosperous future if you take the time to prepare and learn about the financial parts of being an entrepreneur.

Dealing with the Deaths of Family Members

Losing a family member can be hard on your heart and mind, and it can also affect your finances in big ways. It's important to know what financial tasks might come up during this time and be ready to handle them while you're grieving.

Estate Administration

When a family member dies, their assets will need to be taken care of. This process includes paying off any remaining debts, dividing up assets according to the will or state law, and filing the necessary paperwork with the court. If you are chosen to be the executor of the estate, you will be in charge of these jobs.

For help with this process, talk to a lawyer or hire a professional estate planner. They can tell you what paperwork is needed and make sure that the estate is settled according to the law.

Taxes and Wills and Estates

If a family member dies and leaves you money or property, you may have to pay taxes on it. Depending on the amount of the inheritance and the state you live in, you may have to pay inheritance or estate taxes. Talk to a tax expert to make sure you know your responsibilities and are ready to handle any taxes that may come up.

Taking Care of Assets Passed Down

When you get property or investments as a gift, it's important to think about how they fit into your general financial plan. Think about your long-term goals and figure out the best way to handle the assets you received. This could mean selling real estate, reinvesting money you got as a gift, or changing the way you spend.

Changing your own plan

When a family member dies, it can be a good lesson of how important it is to have your own finances in order. Take the time to look over your will, beneficiary names, and any trusts and make sure they are up to date. Make sure you have enough life insurance to protect your family, and talk to them about what you want so there aren't any disagreements or mistakes in the future.

Dealing with a family member's death can be hard and confusing when it comes to money. By getting help from a professional and making plans ahead of time, you can deal with these problems and focus on healing and remembering your loved one.

CHAPTER 9

I hope and pray that after you finish reading this book in its entirety, you, as a young adult, feel empowered, educated, and ready to face the financial challenges that life may throw your way. My goal has always been to give you the tools, knowledge, and confidence you need to make smart choices about your money, whether you're saving for a rainy day, investing in your future, or dealing with big life events.

Financial success is a path that lasts a lifetime. The lessons you learn and habits you form now will help you for many years to come. Remember that success isn't just about how much money you have. It's also about how close you are to reaching your own goals and dreams. Take the time to review and reevaluate your financial plan on a regular basis, adjusting it as needed to fit the changes in your life. This will help you stay on track.

It's important to enjoy your wins, no matter how big or small, and to learn from your mistakes along the way. These things will make you more financially stable and help you grow as a person. And remember that it's never too late to take charge of your financial future. No matter how old you are or what your situation is, you have the power to make a change for the better.

Don't be afraid to ask for help or advice from people you trust as you start this journey. Surround yourself with people who can help you, like family, friends, and financial experts. They can give you advice and motivation as you go. Be open to new ideas and ways of looking at things, and always be ready to learn from those who have gone before you.

I also want you to know that I'll be there for you every step of the way as you work to improve your finances. Don't be afraid to get in touch with me if you have any questions or need more help. More tools and contact information are available on my website, EmpowerYou rPocket.com. You can also follow me on social media at @jimbosuson (Facebook, Instagram and Tiktok) and subscribe to my YouTube page @EmpowerYourPocket, where I share useful tips, insights, and updates. Let's continue to learn, grow, and make our financial lives stronger as a group.

Lastly, I want to stress how important it is to stay true to who you are and what you believe in. Your financial journey will be different from anyone else's, and it's important to make decisions that fit with your own goals and interests. Remember that financial success is about more than just making money. It's also about building a life you're happy with, leaving a legacy you're proud of, and making a difference in the world.

So, here's to your financial future! May it be full of smart choices, ongoing success, and the realization of all your dreams. As you continue to grow and change, try to make the most of every chance you get, and never forget how important it is to invest in yourself and your future.